FINANCIAL WELLNESS FOR WOMEN

I0501654

Easy Guide To Building Wealth, Confidence, And Security

Catherine Moore

Copyright © 2024 Catherine Moore

All rights reserved. No part of this publication may be reproduced, or transmitted in any form or by any means, electronic or mechanical including photocopying, recording or by any information storage and retrieval system without permission in writing from the author.

TABLE OF CONTENTS

INTRODUCTION 8

CHAPTER ONE 12

Foundations of Financial Wellness 12

How Mindset Shifts Helped Emily Save $10,000 16

Setting Financial Goals That Stick 18

SMART Financial Goal Framework 20

CHAPTER TWO 26

Mastering Money Management 26

Easy Budgeting Methods 27

Real-Life Case 31

Tracking Expenses Like a Pro 33

How to Develop Habits for Consistent Tracking 36

CHAPTER THREE 42

Building Wealth from the Ground Up 42

Leveraging Side Hustles and Passive Income Streams . 45

Small Lifestyle Adjustments for Big Savings 47

Understanding Investing Basics 50

Investing for Beginners: Tips to Get Started 53

Secret To Growing Wealth 55

Real Story 55

CHAPTER FOUR 58

Becoming Debt-Free 58

Practical Steps To Becoming Debt Free 64

How to Handle Debt Strategically 65

Methods to Pay Off Debt 67

Real story 70

Staying Debt-Free for the Long Term 73

Building Good Financial Habits 77

CHAPTER FIVE 80

Designing A Life You Love 80

What a "Dream Life" Looks Like 81

Financial Freedom vs. Financial Independence 83

Real Story 84

Living the Dream Today 86

Reassessing Your Spending: Where Can You Add Value? 87

Reinvesting in Yourself 89

Stories of Women Who Transformed Their Finances .. 90

CHAPTER SIX... 94

Avoiding Financial Pitfalls............................. 94

Overspending on Lifestyle Inflation................. 96

Staying Financially Savvy............................. 101

Red Flags to Watch For:............................... 103

Knowing When to Seek Professional Advice........... 104

How to Choose the Right Professional:.............. 106

Long-Term Habits for Financial Safety.............. 107

CHAPTER SEVEN... 110

Creating Generational Wealth........................ 110

Real-Life Story...................................... 113

Key Takeaways.. 114

Estate Planning and Legacy Building................. 115

Educating the Next Generation on Financial Literacy 117

Key Takeaways.. 119

CHAPTER EIGHT.. 120

Your Financial Wellness Journey..................... 120

Goal-Setting Templates.............................. 122

Budget Planning Worksheets.......................... 124

Debt-Tracking Charts.. 125

Key Takeaways.. 126

Reflect and Celebrate Progress................................... 127

Celebrating Small Wins on Your Journey.................. 129

Key Takeaways.. 131

CONCLUSION 134

INTRODUCTION

Imagine waking up one morning and realizing you've spent years juggling bills, working hard, and yet, somehow, you still feel like you're stuck in the same financial place. For Sarah, this was her reality.

At 38, Sarah had a decent job, a home, and a family. But, despite her hard work, she couldn't help but feel overwhelmed by the never-ending cycle of expenses. She'd always put off saving for retirement, and the idea of investing seemed out of reach. Every time she checked her bank account, there was a nagging fear that maybe she wasn't doing enough—or that she had missed the boat entirely. Her dreams of financial security seemed increasingly distant.

Does this sound familiar?

You're not alone. Women like Sarah, and countless others, face unique financial challenges—many of which are tied to gender. From the gender pay gap and career breaks for care-giving to societal pressures around spending and saving, women often find themselves playing catch-up when it comes to financial independence.

But what if I told you that financial wellness isn't an impossible dream? What if I told you that you could break free from financial uncertainty, build wealth, and take control of your future—no matter where you're starting from?

This book is for you—the woman who is ready to rewrite her financial story. The woman who wants to build a life of independence, confidence, and security, without being overwhelmed by debt or ruled by financial anxiety. You'll learn how to navigate the myths that have held you back, like "I'm too late to start saving" or "Investing is only for the wealthy." These beliefs only create roadblocks, but together, we'll break them down and build a new, empowering mindset.

Through relatable stories, actionable steps, and real-life examples, you'll gain the confidence to tackle your finances head-on. Once you are done going through this guide, you'll be able to:

- Take control of your financial future and make informed decisions that support your goals
- Build financial independence so that you're not dependent on anyone else for your security

- Create a realistic plan for eliminating debt and stop feeling burdened by financial obligations
- Design a life you love, whether it's achieving a dream vacation, retiring early, or simply having the peace of mind that comes with financial stability

The journey to financial freedom doesn't have to be overwhelming. You don't need to have a background in finance to understand and apply the principles in this book. It's about taking small, consistent steps that add up over time, and most importantly—starting right now.

This guide will show you how to make your money work for you, give you the tools to make better financial decisions, and empower you to reach a place where you're not just surviving, but thriving.

Are you ready to start? Let's get to work.

11 | Catherine Moore

CHAPTER ONE

Foundations of Financial Wellness

Money isn't just about numbers; it's deeply connected to how we think, feel, and act in relation to it. Everyone has a relationship with money, but most of us don't stop to understand it. That's a mistake because our attitudes toward money can significantly influence how we handle it—whether we save, spend, or even think about it at all.

Money is more than a tool for buying things; it's tied to our emotions, values, and beliefs. For example, do you see money as a source of stress? Or do you view it as a tool for freedom and opportunity? Your mindset plays a huge role in determining your financial habits, and it's important to assess this relationship early on in your journey to financial wellness.

The first step is to recognize your personal money patterns. Do you tend to spend impulsively? Do you avoid looking at your bank balance because it makes you anxious? Understanding your relationship with money will give you the insight you need to make better decisions moving forward.

Identifying Your Money Mindset

Your money mindset refers to the beliefs and attitudes you have about money. These beliefs can be shaped by your upbringing, personal experiences, and society's messages about wealth. Your mindset can either limit you or empower you to make smart financial decisions. Here are some common money mindsets:

Scarcity Mindset: This mindset is rooted in the belief that there's never enough money. People with a scarcity mindset often feel anxious about money, leading them to hoard, overspend, or avoid financial planning altogether. They may worry constantly about running out of money, even when they have enough.

Abundance Mindset: Those with an abundance mindset believe that there are always opportunities to create wealth and that money is a tool for growth and freedom. They are more likely to invest in themselves, save for the future, and make confident financial decisions.

Money Avoidance: People with this mindset tend to ignore money matters altogether. They might avoid looking at their bank accounts or making financial decisions out of fear or confusion. This mindset can lead to neglecting savings, ignoring debt, and missing opportunities to build wealth.

Money Worship: This mindset sees money as the ultimate goal. People who worship money might equate their self-worth with their financial success. While they might be motivated to earn more, they may also struggle with spending and materialism.

It's important to identify your money mindset because it influences how you handle financial stress, make decisions, and even how comfortable you feel with your finances. Understanding your mindset is the first step toward improving your financial health.

Overcoming Financial Anxiety

Money-related anxiety is a common experience. Whether it's worrying about bills, student loans, or the fear of never being able to save enough for retirement, financial anxiety can hold you back from reaching your financial goals.

But the good news is: you can overcome financial anxiety. Here are some steps to help you take control:

Acknowledge Your Fears: The first step is acknowledging the fear you feel around money. Are you worried about not having enough to retire? Are you stressed by debt? Once you recognize the source of your anxiety, you can begin addressing it head-on.

Break It Down: Anxiety often comes from feeling overwhelmed. Break down your financial challenges into smaller, manageable steps. For example, instead of thinking about saving for retirement as one big goal, start by setting a goal to save $50 a month. As you accomplish small goals, your anxiety will lessen.

Focus on What You Can Control: There will always be things outside of your control—like economic downturns or unexpected medical expenses. Instead of stressing about these unknowns, focus on what you can control: budgeting, saving, and planning for the future.

Get Educated: Sometimes, financial anxiety comes from not understanding how money works. As you deepen your knowledge of personal finance, your confidence will grow.

Begin with mastering the fundamentals of budgeting, saving, and investing. Knowledge is power.

Surround Yourself with Support: You don't have to face financial anxiety alone. Turn to friends, family, or a financial advisor for guidance and support. Having someone to talk to about money can make it less intimidating and more manageable.

How Mindset Shifts Helped Emily Save $10,000

Let's take a look at Emily, a woman who, like many others, struggled with money anxiety. Emily was 30 years old and had always lived paycheck to paycheck. She never seemed to have enough money for the things she wanted or needed. Every time a bill came, she felt anxious and overwhelmed.

Emily had always believed that she just wasn't good with money. She grew up in a household where money was a constant source of stress, and she carried that fear into her adulthood. For years, she had a scarcity mindset—always fearing that she wouldn't have enough, and so she'd either overspend or avoid saving altogether.

Then, one day, Emily had a realization: she couldn't keep living like this. She was tired of the stress and anxiety that came with her finances. So, she decided to shift her mindset.

First, she took small steps to address her fears. She began by tracking her spending to understand where her money was going. She was shocked to find that a large portion of her spending was on small, impulsive purchases—things she didn't even need. Once she had this insight, Emily started setting clear financial goals.

Instead of focusing on the "big picture" of saving for retirement or paying off all of her debt, Emily focused on small, attainable goals. She started by saving $100 a month. As she gained confidence and saw her savings grow, she increased the amount.

In just one year, Emily saved $10,000—an amount she never thought was possible. The key to her success was her mindset shift. By moving from a scarcity mindset to an abundance mindset, Emily stopped feeling trapped by her finances. She felt empowered to make choices that aligned with her goals.

Emily's story shows that no matter where you start, you have the power to change your financial future. It all begins with understanding your relationship with money and shifting your mindset to one of abundance and possibility.

Setting Financial Goals That Stick

Setting financial goals is the foundation of any successful financial journey. Without clear goals, it's easy to drift from month to month, unsure of where your money is going or why you're saving in the first place. Financial goals act as a roadmap—helping you stay focused, motivated, and on track.

The key to successful financial goal-setting is not just about deciding what you want to achieve. It's about breaking down your goals into manageable steps, keeping yourself accountable, and adjusting along the way when life happens. Financial goals help you create a sense of purpose around your money, turning it from a stressor into a tool for creating the life you want.

Short-Term vs. Long-Term Goals

When it comes to financial goals, they generally fall into two categories: short-term and long-term.

Short-Term Goals

Short-term goals are those you aim to achieve within the next few months to a year. These goals are typically smaller, more immediate, and easier to measure. They might include building an emergency fund, paying off a small debt, or saving for a vacation. Short-term goals provide quick wins that boost your confidence and motivation.

Examples of short-term goals:

- Saving $500 for an emergency fund.
- Clearing a credit card balance within 3 months.
- Setting aside money for a new appliance or car repair.

Long-Term Goals

Long-term goals are those you plan to achieve in a year or more. These are usually bigger goals that require sustained effort and planning, like buying a home, building retirement savings, or paying off a mortgage. Long-term goals are often tied to significant life changes, so it's important to keep your eye on the prize and take consistent steps toward them.

Examples of long-term goals:

- Saving for retirement.
- Buying a home in the next 5 years.
- Clearing student loans in 10 years.

Both short-term and long-term goals are equally important. Short-term goals help you stay motivated and create positive financial habits, while long-term goals help you build a secure future. Together, they create a balanced approach to financial wellness.

SMART Financial Goal Framework

The SMART framework is a powerful tool for turning vague, wishful thinking into concrete, actionable plans. SMART stands for Specific, Measurable, Achievable, Relevant, and Time-bound—five key elements that help you set goals that are clear, actionable, and achievable. Let's break it down:

Specific

Your goal should be clear and well-defined. Instead of saying, "I want to save money," say, "I want to save $1,000 for an emergency fund." The more specific your goal, the easier it will be to stay focused.

Measurable

You need a way to track your progress. A measurable goal allows you to see how close you are to your objective. In our example, the goal is saving $1,000—this is a specific amount you can measure as you go.

Achievable

Your goal should be realistic, based on your current financial situation. If you're just starting to save, setting a goal of saving $10,000 in three months might not be achievable. But saving $1,000 in three months might be. Be sure your goal is within reach, so you stay motivated.

Relevant

Your goal should align with your larger financial priorities. Ask yourself: Is this goal in line with my bigger financial picture? For example, if your priority is to pay off high-interest debt, saving for a vacation may not be as relevant in the short term.

Time-bound

Set a clear deadline for achieving your goal. This helps create a sense of urgency and allows you to stay on track.

For example, "I will save $1,000 in the next three months" is a time-bound goal that gives you a clear timeline.

By using the SMART framework, you'll have a clear path to follow, which will make your financial goals feel more attainable and less overwhelming.

Sarah's Journey from Living Paycheck-to-Paycheck to Owning Her First Home

Let's look at Sarah, a woman in her early 30s who had struggled with money for years. She was living paycheck-to-paycheck, using credit cards to cover everyday expenses, and didn't have any savings to speak of. Sarah felt stuck and overwhelmed by her financial situation.

But one day, she realized something important: she needed to make a change. She decided to get serious about her finances and set a goal of buying her first home in the next 5 years. She was determined to take control of her money and stop living paycheck-to-paycheck.

To start, Sarah followed the SMART framework to set her goals:

Specific: Sarah's specific goal was to save $20,000 for a down payment on a house.

Measurable: She broke this down into monthly savings targets. She calculated that she needed to save about $400 per month to reach her goal.

Achievable: Sarah evaluated her monthly expenses and realized she could cut back on non-essential spending, like dining out and subscription services, which gave her the extra $400 per month she needed.

Relevant: Owning a home was a key part of Sarah's long-term goals. She wanted financial stability, and owning a home was a natural next step in her journey.

Time-bound: Sarah set a timeline of 5 years to reach her $20,000 goal for the down payment, giving herself a clear deadline to work toward.

Over the next few months, Sarah stuck to her plan. She made a few sacrifices, like reducing her eating-out budget and shopping for deals. As she saw her savings grow, she felt more confident and motivated. By the end of the year, she had saved $4,800—a huge accomplishment.

Sarah also started making small adjustments in other areas of her life, like refinancing high-interest debt and investing in a retirement plan. By staying consistent and revisiting her goals regularly, Sarah eventually reached her $20,000 down payment target in just over 4 years.

When Sarah finally walked through the doors of her new home, she felt a deep sense of pride and relief. She had gone from struggling with money to becoming a homeowner, all because she set clear financial goals, used the SMART framework, and took consistent action.

Turning Goals into Reality

Sarah's story shows us that no matter where you start, setting clear financial goals—whether short-term or long-term—helps turn dreams into reality. By using the SMART framework, you can create goals that are specific, measurable, achievable, relevant, and time-bound, putting you in control of your financial future.

Now it's your turn. Start by thinking about your own financial goals. What are they things you would want to achieve for the coming year? The next five years? The next ten? Remember, no goal is too small, and every step forward brings you closer to financial freedom.

CHAPTER TWO

Mastering Money Management

Managing your money effectively begins with understanding where your money goes. This is where budgeting comes in. Budgeting is simply the process of allocating your income toward your expenses, savings, and goals. It may sound simple, but many people struggle to stick to a budget because they either don't set one at all or they fail to follow it consistently.

A budget is essential for financial wellness. It helps you:

- Keep track of how much you're earning versus how much you're spending.
- Set and prioritize your financial goals.
- Avoid overspending and debt accumulation.
- Create a clear path toward saving and financial independence.

But how can you create a budget that truly works? It starts with knowing your income, your necessary expenses (like rent, utilities, food), and your discretionary spending (like entertainment and shopping). Once you know where your money is going, you can make informed decisions about where to cut back and how to save more.

To stick to a budget, you must be committed and realistic. A budget is a guide, not a set of strict rules. Life happens—unexpected expenses come up, and spending habits can fluctuate. The goal is not perfection but consistency. Review your budget regularly, tweak it when necessary, and hold yourself accountable. This will pave the way for success that will last.

Easy Budgeting Methods

There are several popular methods to create a budget that works for you. Two of the most common methods are the 50/30/20 Rule and Zero-Based Budgeting. Let's break them down:

The 50/30/20 Rule

This is one of the easiest and most straightforward budgeting methods. The idea is simple: divide your after-tax income into three categories:

50% of costs are non-negotiable and include things like rent, utilities, groceries, insurance, and transportation.

30% Wants: These are things you enjoy but can live without, like dining out, entertainment, shopping, and subscriptions.

20% Savings and Debt Repayment: This is the money you put toward your emergency fund, retirement, and paying off debt.

The 50/30/20 Rule is ideal for those who want a basic, no-fuss method for managing their money. It helps ensure that your essential needs are covered while also prioritizing savings and debt repayment. If you find that you're spending more than 30% on "wants," it's time to reassess and make adjustments.

Zero-Based Budgeting

Zero-Based Budgeting (ZBB) is a method where every dollar of your income is assigned a specific job. The goal is to have zero money left at the end of the month, meaning every dollar is accounted for. Unlike the 50/30/20 Rule, which has set categories, Zero-Based Budgeting starts from scratch each month.

Here's how it works:

- List all your sources of income.
- List every single expense, including fixed (rent, utilities) and variable (groceries, entertainment).
- Set aside enough money from your income to pay for all of these costs.
- If you have leftover money, it goes toward savings or debt repayment.

Zero-Based Budgeting is ideal for people who want complete control over every dollar they spend. It requires more tracking and effort than the 50/30/20 Rule but can be a great way to make sure every cent counts toward your goals.

Typical Budgeting Errors and Their Solutions

Budgeting can be challenging, especially if you're just starting. Here are some common mistakes people make and tips on how to fix them:

Not Tracking Your Spending

The Mistake: You create a budget but fail to track where your money is actually going. Without tracking, it's easy to lose sight of your financial goals and overspend.

How to Fix It: Use budgeting apps like Mint or YNAB (You Need a Budget) to track your spending automatically. Or, you can go old school and keep a spending journal. Reviewing your spending on a regular basis enables you to stay on course and make any modifications.

Underestimating Expenses

The Mistake: You think you'll spend less on groceries or entertainment than you actually do, leading to budget shortfalls.

How to Fix It: Be honest with yourself about your spending habits. Look at past bills and spending trends to estimate your expenses more accurately. If you're not sure how much to allocate for something, err on the side of caution and give yourself a little buffer.

Not Prioritizing Savings

The Mistake: You focus on paying bills and living expenses first, leaving no room for savings or emergency funds.

How to Fix It: Treat savings as a non-negotiable expense. As soon as you receive your income, allocate money to savings before anything else. Streamline your savings by automating transfers for simplicity.

Ignoring Debt Repayment

The Mistake: You might allocate money to your savings but neglect to pay off high-interest debt, such as credit cards, leading to increased financial strain.

How to Fix It: Prioritize paying off high-interest debt first. After that, focus on saving for your future. There's no point in saving if your debt is growing faster than your savings.

Real-Life Case

Let's talk about Rebecca, a woman who was struggling to keep her spending in check. She lived paycheck-to-paycheck and found herself using credit cards more than she wanted to. She realized that in order to save for her future, she needed to take control of her finances and start budgeting.

Rebecca decided to use the 50/30/20 Rule to structure her budget. She knew she needed to make some sacrifices, but she also wanted to enjoy life. Here's how she made it work:

Tracking Spending: The first step Rebecca took was tracking every penny. She downloaded a budgeting app and spent a few weeks logging all her expenses. She quickly realized that her "wants" category (eating out, subscription services, and shopping) was eating up a lot of her income.

Cutting Back on "Wants": Rebecca wasn't willing to eliminate all of her pleasures, but she made smarter choices. She started meal prepping for the week, cutting down on take-out, and paused a few unnecessary subscriptions. She also swapped expensive weekend activities for free or low-cost alternatives like hiking or visiting local parks.

Reducing Unnecessary Bills: Rebecca contacted her service providers to negotiate lower rates for her cable and phone plan. She also switched to a more affordable internet package, saving an extra $100 a month.

By being mindful and following her 50/30/20 budget, Rebecca was able to cut back by $500 every month. This allowed her to build an emergency fund, pay down debt, and start saving for a vacation she'd always dreamed of. The best part? She didn't feel deprived. She was still able to enjoy life—just in a more intentional, thoughtful way.

Money management is about making informed, intentional decisions with your money. Whether you follow the 50/30/20 Rule or Zero-Based Budgeting, the key is to build a system that works for you. By tracking your spending, setting realistic goals, and avoiding common budgeting mistakes, you'll take control of your finances and move toward a more secure and fulfilling future.

Rebecca's story shows us that budgeting isn't about restriction—it's about creating space for the things that matter most. Start small, be consistent, and remember that every dollar counts toward your future financial wellness.

Tracking Expenses Like a Pro

In today's digital age, managing your expenses doesn't have to be a complicated task. Gone are the days of sifting through receipts and manually entering data into spreadsheets. With the right tools, tracking your expenses can be quick, efficient, and even enjoyable.

Several apps and tools can help streamline this process, allowing you to focus on your goals without getting bogged down by the details. The following are highly recommended:

Mint

Mint is a popular, free budgeting app that automatically tracks your expenses by syncing with your bank accounts, credit cards, and bills. It categorizes your spending, provides insights into your spending habits, and even alerts you when bills are due.

Jessica, a 32-year-old freelancer, struggled to track her income and expenses with multiple sources of payment. After downloading Mint, she synced her accounts and instantly had a clear view of where her money was going. Mint's visual graphs helped her realize that she was spending too much on dining out and subscriptions, motivating her to cut back.

YNAB (You Need A Budget)

YNAB focuses on helping users assign every dollar to a specific job, ensuring that all your income is used toward your goals. It's a paid app but offers in-depth features that help you plan, track, and adjust your spending.

Sarah, a teacher with student loans, used YNAB to prioritize her spending. By assigning money to her savings and debt repayments before anything else, she found that she could save $200 more per month while still covering her living expenses.

EveryDollar

Created by financial expert Dave Ramsey, EveryDollar is a budgeting tool that follows the zero-based budgeting method. It allows you to set up a detailed budget, track expenses, and stick to your goals.

Chris and Maria, a married couple, used EveryDollar to tackle their debt. They set up a detailed budget and categorized each expense. The app helped them stick to their budget, ultimately paying off $10,000 in credit card debt within a year.

GoodBudget

GoodBudget is an envelope budgeting app that helps you plan and track your spending by setting aside "envelopes" for each spending category. It's perfect for people who like the traditional envelope method but want to manage it digitally.

Mark, a small business owner, needed a system to manage his business and personal expenses. He used GoodBudget to set aside envelopes for groceries, gas, and savings. This visual method kept him disciplined and on track.

Each of these tools can help simplify expense tracking, but choosing the right one depends on your preferences. Do you want something automated and hands-off, or do you prefer a more hands-on approach to assigning funds?

How to Develop Habits for Consistent Tracking

Now that you have the right tools at your disposal, the next step is to develop the habit of consistently tracking your expenses. The key to successful expense management is routine—without it, even the best tools can fall by the wayside. Here are a few strategies to help you build this habit:

Set a Daily Check-In Time

Consistency is crucial. Designate a specific time each day (perhaps during your morning coffee or before bed) to review your expenses. This daily ritual will keep you aware of your spending and prevent any surprises at the end of the month.

Real-life example: Lucy, a busy single mom, carved out 10 minutes each morning to review her transactions. By making it a non-negotiable part of her day, she ensured she stayed on top of her finances without feeling overwhelmed.

Automate Whenever Possible

The less manual effort required, the more likely you are to stay on track. Set up automatic syncing for your bank accounts and credit cards with your expense tracking apps, so the data is updated in real-time.

Tim, a college student, struggled with remembering to log his spending after nights out with friends. After setting up automatic sync with Mint, his transactions were logged automatically, which made it much easier to stay on top of his finances.

Review Weekly to Stay on Track

A weekly review allows you to make mid-course corrections. If you notice you're overspending on a category, you can adjust before it gets out of hand.

Maria, a freelance graphic designer, did a weekly check-in to ensure she was hitting her savings targets. She noticed that she was spending more on software subscriptions than she had planned, so she adjusted her budget and cut back.

Celebrate Small Wins

Tracking your expenses can feel like a lot of work, so it's important to celebrate small victories. When you manage to stick to your budget or reduce an unnecessary expense, take a moment to acknowledge your efforts.

After tracking her expenses for three consecutive weeks, Lisa treated herself to a small reward—a day out with friends. This positive reinforcement motivated her to stay consistent with her tracking habits.

Make It a Family or Team Activity

If you share finances with a partner or a family, involving everyone in the tracking process can help everyone stay aligned with your financial goals. This ensures accountability and teamwork in achieving your goals.

Sean and Emily, a couple with young children, made expense tracking a family activity. They used YNAB and reviewed their expenses together each Sunday, which helped them stay on the same page financially. Their children were also encouraged to contribute by saving their pocket money.

Tracking your expenses doesn't need to be a daunting task. With the right tools and a commitment to consistency, you can stay on top of your finances and ensure that you're always moving toward your goals. By developing small, manageable habits and regularly reviewing your spending, you'll have the control and clarity you need to master your money.

Whether you choose an app that syncs automatically, or you prefer a more hands-on approach, the key to success is making tracking a non-negotiable part of your routine. Just like any other habit, the more you practice, the easier it becomes. And before you know it, tracking expenses will be second nature, helping you move closer to your financial dreams every single day.

CHAPTER THREE

Building Wealth from the Ground Up

Building wealth isn't a "get rich quick" endeavour. It's a gradual process that requires patience, discipline, and a mindset that's focused on long-term goals. The great thing is, you don't need to start with a fortune to build wealth. In fact, most people who build significant wealth do so by starting small and making steady progress over time.

Easy Wealth-Building Strategies

Building wealth doesn't require a high-paying job or secret knowledge. What it takes is consistency, smart choices, and a plan to make your money work for you. Here are some simple yet effective strategies to start building wealth today.

Start Saving Early, Even If It's Small: The earlier you start saving, the more time your money has to grow. Time, especially when it comes to compound interest, is one of the most powerful tools you have in building wealth. Even if you can only afford to save a small amount at first, starting early gives your savings the time they need to accumulate.

Let's say you're in your twenties and you can only set aside $50 a month. Over the next 10 years, that might not seem like much. But with compound interest working in your favour, that $50 could grow into thousands. And if you increase your savings over time as your income grows, that initial $50 could turn into a sizable nest egg by the time you're ready to retire.

Automate Your Savings: One of the best ways to make sure you actually save is to make it automatic. Automating your savings means setting up automatic transfers from your checking account to your savings or investment account. By treating savings as a "bill" that you pay yourself, it becomes non-negotiable. You'll be less likely to use it for other expenses.

Set up an automatic transfer that happens the day after your paycheck comes in. You won't miss it, and over time, you'll be amazed at how quickly it adds up.

Maximize Retirement Accounts: If your employer offers a 401(k) plan, it's one of the easiest ways to save for the future. Many employers offer matching contributions, providing you with essentially free money. Don't leave that on the table.

Strive to contribute enough to maximize your employer's matching contributions. If they match 3% of your salary, for example, that's 3% that's added to your retirement account without you having to do anything. It's an immediate return on your investment.

Invest Wisely: Investing is a key part of building wealth. Putting your money into assets like stocks, bonds, or mutual funds allows it to grow at a faster rate than it would in a traditional savings account. When you start investing early enough, your investment will have more time to grow.

If you're new to investing, you don't need to jump into complex investments right away. Look into low-cost index funds or exchange-traded funds (ETFs) that provide broad market diversification. These funds allow you to invest in many companies at once, minimizing your risk while still giving you the potential for growth.

Leveraging Side Hustles and Passive Income Streams

In addition to saving and investing, finding ways to earn more money is another powerful way to build wealth. Whether it's starting a side hustle or creating passive income streams, these additional sources of income can help accelerate your wealth-building.

Side Hustles: Turning Passion Into Profit

A side hustle is any work you do in addition to your full-time job to earn extra money. Many people start side hustles to pay off debt, save for a specific goal, or just increase their financial security. A side hustle doesn't have to be a huge time commitment—often, it's about using your skills and interests to make extra cash.

Think about what you already enjoy doing or what skills you have. Are you good at writing? Freelance writing might be a great side hustle. Love taking photos? You could sell your images online. The key is to leverage your interests and skills in ways that bring in extra income.

Passive Income: Earning While You Sleep

Unlike side hustles, passive income doesn't require constant effort. Once you've set things up, passive income streams allow you to earn money with little ongoing work. Examples of passive income include rental properties, dividends from stocks, or royalties from content you create, like e-books or courses.

Start small with passive income by investing in dividend-paying stocks or using platforms like Airbnb to rent out a room in your home. Over time, these small passive income sources can grow into a reliable revenue stream.

Creating an Online Business

The internet has made it easier than ever to start a business with low overhead costs. Whether you're selling a physical product or offering a service, online businesses are a great way to supplement your income and build wealth.

Explore online marketplaces like Etsy, eBay, or even social media platforms like Instagram to sell products. If you have expertise in a specific area, you could create an online course, start a YouTube channel, or even write an e-book.

The key is consistency and dedication to building your online presence.

Small Lifestyle Adjustments for Big Savings

Building wealth is about making smart choices with your money, and sometimes, those choices can come from adjusting your lifestyle. Small changes in your daily habits can add up over time, leading to significant savings that you can then invest or save for bigger goals.

Cutting Unnecessary Expenses

You'd be surprised how much money you're throwing away on subscriptions and services that you don't use. Start by reviewing your monthly expenses and eliminating things that don't add value to your life.

Take a look at all your subscriptions—streaming services, magazines, gym memberships—and cancel anything you're not actively using. This could free up hundreds of dollars a year, which you can then put toward savings or investments.

Cooking at Home

Eating out is a major expense that many people don't realize is adding up. By cooking meals at home, you not only save money but also have more control over what you're eating.

Planning meals and cooking in bulk can help you save both time and money. Set aside one day a week to prepare meals in advance, and you'll be surprised at how much you can save by avoiding takeout and dining out.

Downsizing Where Possible

Whether it's your home, car, or lifestyle, downsizing can be a game-changer. If you're living in a larger home than you need or driving a car that's more expensive than necessary, consider making adjustments to save money.

If you're paying for a large apartment or house, think about moving to a smaller, more affordable space. The money saved could go into investments or help pay off debt.

Example: How Jane Turned a Hobby Into a $30,000 Side Business

Jane was an elementary school teacher who loved making jewellery in her spare time. What started as a hobby quickly became a small business after she decided to sell her designs on Etsy. She initially made just a few sales, but as her skills grew, she gained more attention online. Over time, Jane added social media marketing to her efforts, and her sales took off.

Within a year, Jane's side business was bringing in over $30,000 a year. The extra income allowed her to pay off credit card debt, start investing, and save for future goals. What's even better, Jane didn't quit her day job. The extra money from her side business allowed her to achieve financial goals without feeling overwhelmed by the demands of a full-time job.

Wealth-building is a marathon, not a sprint. But by starting now, implementing these strategies, and sticking to your plan, you'll be well on your way to financial security. Whether you're automating savings, taking on a side hustle, or making small lifestyle changes, every step you take brings you closer to your goals.

Remember, the path to building wealth doesn't require drastic changes overnight. It's about consistently making better choices, using your time and resources wisely, and staying focused on your long-term financial success. You have the power to start building wealth from the ground up, and it all begins today.

Understanding Investing Basics

Investing can be intimidating, especially if you are new in it. But here's the truth: you don't need to be a financial expert to start building wealth through investments. In fact, learning the basics of investing can put you on a path toward achieving your financial goals, whether that's saving for retirement, building an emergency fund, or securing your children's future.

Types of Investments

When you hear people talk about investing, they're often referring to three main types of investments: stocks, bonds, and mutual funds. Each of these has its own set of characteristics and risk levels, but they all have the potential to grow your money over time.

Stocks: Ownership in a Company

When you buy a stock, you're acquiring a small share of ownership in a company. The value of your stock can rise or fall depending on the company's performance. Stocks generally offer the highest potential for growth, but they can also be the riskiest because their value can fluctuate significantly.

Begin by investing in established companies with a track record of consistent performance. This is often called investing in "blue-chip" stocks. Companies like Apple, Microsoft, or Coca-Cola are examples of businesses that tend to be more stable over the long term.

Bonds: Lending Money to Governments or Companies

When you buy a bond, you're essentially lending money to the government or a corporation for a certain period of time. In exchange, the issuer of the bond promises to pay you interest over the life of the bond and return your principal when the bond matures. Bonds are generally considered less risky than stocks, but they offer lower returns.

Government bonds (like U.S. Treasury bonds) are usually very safe because they're backed by the government. If you're just getting started with investing and want something low-risk, consider bonds as a way to add stability to your portfolio.

Mutual Funds: A Pool of Investments

A mutual fund combines money from multiple investors to invest in a diverse range of assets, such as stocks, bonds, real estate, or other securities. This allows investors to diversify their portfolios without having to pick individual stocks or bonds themselves. Mutual funds are great for beginners because they offer diversification and are professionally managed.

Consider index funds or exchange-traded funds (ETFs), which are types of mutual funds that track the performance of a specific market index, like the S&P 500. These funds provide broad market exposure, reduce risk, and often have lower fees than actively managed funds.

Investing for Beginners: Tips to Get Started

So, now that you know about the different types of investments, how do you actually get started? Here are some practical tips to help you take the first step toward building your investment portfolio.

Start Small and Be Consistent

You don't need a large amount of money to begin investing. In fact, many brokers allow you to open an account with as little as $100 or even less. The key is to begin with small amounts and invest consistently. Even a modest monthly contribution can grow over time.

If you can, automate your investments. Set up a direct deposit or automatic transfer into your investment account so that you're consistently investing without having to think about it.

Use Low-Cost Investment Platforms

There are plenty of online platforms and apps designed to make investing easier and more affordable for beginners. Many of these platforms offer low or no fees, making it easier to start investing without worrying about high costs eating into your returns.

Look for robo-advisors, which are automated platforms that manage your investments based on your goals and risk tolerance. Many popular robo-advisors, like Betterment or Wealthfront, offer diversified portfolios with low management fees.

Focus on Long-Term Goals

Investing isn't a "get rich quick" activity. It's about allowing your money to grow and work for you over time. Keep your long-term goals in mind, and don't get discouraged by short-term market fluctuations. The more time your money has to grow, the more it can benefit from compounding interest.

Set clear goals for your investments, whether it's for retirement, buying a house, or funding your children's education. Use those goals to stay focused and avoid making emotional decisions when the market dips.

Secret To Growing Wealth

Interest on interest is one of the most powerful forces in investing. It's the process by which the interest you earn on your investment gets reinvested, and then you earn interest on that interest. Over time, compounding can turn even a small investment into a large sum.

The key to benefiting from compounding is time. The more time your money has to compound, the greater the impact.

Let's say you invest $100 each month into a retirement account that earns an average annual return of 7%. After 20 years, your $100 monthly investment would grow to over $50,000, thanks to the power of compounding. If you wait even longer, the amount grows even more dramatically.

Real Story

How a $50 Monthly Investment Grew Into a College Fund

Meet Sarah, a mom who wanted to make sure her son had the opportunity to attend college without burdening him with debt. At the time, Sarah wasn't making much money, and she wasn't sure how she could ever save enough to cover the rising costs of tuition. But she started small.

Sarah decided to invest $50 a month in a low-cost index fund. At first, it didn't seem like much. But over time, with steady contributions and the power of compounding, Sarah's small monthly investment grew. After 10 years, her $50 monthly contributions turned into a college fund worth more than $8,000.

When her son graduated from high school, Sarah was able to use the fund to cover a significant portion of his college tuition. By starting early and staying committed to regular investments, she had secured her child's future without having to sacrifice her own financial stability.

Investing doesn't have to be complicated. By understanding the basics—stocks, bonds, mutual funds—and following simple tips for beginners, you can start building your wealth right now. The power of compounding interest means that even small investments can grow over time, and with consistency, you'll be well on your way to reaching your financial goals.

Whether you're saving for retirement, your child's education, or just building your financial security, now is the perfect time to take that first step. With the right knowledge and a solid plan, you can turn your small investments today into a brighter financial future tomorrow.

CHAPTER FOUR

Becoming Debt-Free

Becoming debt-free is a journey, and while it may seem overwhelming at first, it's absolutely achievable with the right mindset, strategy, and patience. Many women find themselves struggling with debt at different points in their lives. Whether it's from credit card mismanagement, student loans, or unexpected medical expenses, debt can feel like an insurmountable obstacle. But the good news is, with the right steps, it can be tackled and eliminated.

How Debt Happens

Debt doesn't happen overnight. For most people, it builds slowly over time, often starting with small purchases or unexpected expenses. Here are the most common ways debt sneaks up:

Living Beyond Your Means: When you consistently spend more than you earn, whether it's through impulse purchases or lifestyle inflation, debt begins to accumulate.

This often happens when there's little distinction between "wants" and "needs," and budgeting isn't a priority.

High-Interest Credit Cards: Credit cards are often marketed as a convenient way to purchase now and pay later. However, high-interest rates can quickly turn small balances into large debts if they're not paid off in full each month.

Student Loans: While student loans can be an investment in your future, they can also become overwhelming if not managed wisely. The high costs of tuition, combined with low-paying entry-level jobs, can make paying off student loans seem impossible.

Medical Emergencies: Without an emergency fund, a sudden medical issue can lead to significant debt. Even with insurance, deductibles, copayments, and uncovered procedures can result in unexpected costs.

Lack of Emergency Savings: Without a financial safety net, life's inevitable surprises—car repairs, job loss, or even family emergencies—can result in relying on credit, taking out loans, or borrowing from family and friends.

Real-Life Examples:

Let's take a closer look at a few real-life scenarios to understand how easily debt can spiral out of control—and more importantly, how it can be fixed.

1. Credit Card Mismanagement: Lisa's $15,000 Debt Spiral

Lisa's story starts like many others: a few impulse purchases here, a couple of splurges there, and suddenly, she was stuck in credit card debt. Lisa used her credit cards for everything from groceries to vacations, and without a clear understanding of her interest rates and monthly payments, she began to carry a balance from month to month.

Her $2,000 in credit card debt quickly ballooned to $15,000 after years of making minimum payments that only covered the interest. She felt trapped, as every time she paid down a little of the balance, new charges popped up. The high interest rates on her credit cards only made the problem worse, leading to a never-ending cycle of debt. Lisa realized that the only way to get out was to stop adding to the debt and focus on paying it down in a strategic way.

Lessons to learn:

- Don't Carry a Balance: If possible, pay off your credit card bill in full each month to avoid interest charges.
- High Interest = Big Problems: Focus on paying off the credit card with the highest interest rate first, a strategy known as the debt avalanche method.
- Start Budgeting: Keep track of where your money is going. Without a budget, it's easy to lose sight of how much debt you've accumulated.

2. Student Loans: Anna's $80,000 in Student Debt

Anna, a college graduate, entered the workforce with high hopes and big dreams. But reality hit hard when she looked at her student loan balance—$80,000. While she was able to secure a decent job out of college, her monthly student loan payments of $1,000 quickly ate into her salary, leaving her little room for savings or financial freedom.

For years, Anna made only the minimum payments on her loans, watching as the balance barely budged. The interest kept adding up, making it feel like she was getting nowhere. It wasn't until she sat down and calculated the long-term cost of her loans that she realized the importance of paying more than the minimum.

Lessons to learn:

- **Refinance to Lower Interest Rates:** If you're eligible, refinancing your student loans can lower your interest rates, reducing the amount of interest you'll pay over time.

- **Pay More Than the Minimum:** By paying more than the minimum, Anna was able to pay down the principal faster, reducing the total interest she'd pay in the long run.

- **Consider Loan Forgiveness:** Some careers, like teaching or working in public service, offer loan forgiveness after a set number of years. Anna researched her options and found ways to make her student loans more manageable.

3. Medical Emergencies Without an Emergency Fund

When Rachel's car broke down and her insurance didn't cover the full cost of repairs, she found herself in a tough spot. A few weeks later, her child had to undergo a minor but costly medical procedure, and Rachel had to rely on her credit cards to cover the expenses. Without an emergency fund, every unexpected cost became an immediate source of stress and debt.

By the time Rachel realized how much debt she had accumulated, her credit card balances had reached over $8,000. She was paying interest on both car repairs and medical bills, and the cycle seemed impossible to break.

Lessons to learn:

- Build an Emergency Fund First: Having an emergency fund can prevent you from relying on credit when life's unexpected expenses arise. Target saving at least three to six months' worth of living expenses.

- Negotiate Medical Bills: Rachel learned that medical providers often offer payment plans or discounts for paying upfront. Don't be afraid to ask.

- Health Insurance Matters: While she couldn't control all medical costs, Rachel also learned to carefully evaluate health insurance options to avoid high out-of-pocket costs in the future.

Practical Steps To Becoming Debt Free

Debt can feel like a weight that's impossible to lift, but the good news is that you can regain control. Here's a step-by-step plan to help you work towards becoming debt-free:

- Stop adding to the Debt: The first step to getting debt-free is to stop making new charges. Refrain from unnecessary spending and focus on paying off what you owe.

- Create a Debt Repayment Plan: Choose one of the following strategies to pay off your debt:

- Debt Snowball: Focus on paying off the smallest debt first, then move on to the next. This method builds momentum as you see your debts disappearing.

- Debt Avalanche: Prioritize paying off the debt with the highest interest rate first. This saves you more money in the long run, as you'll pay less interest.

- Find Extra Income: Consider side gigs, freelancing, or selling items you no longer need to increase your monthly payments. Every additional dollar you contribute to your debt can have a significant impact.

- Seek Professional Help: If your debt feels overwhelming, consider working with a financial advisor or credit counsellor who can help you create a personalized debt repayment strategy.

Becoming debt-free is a process, but it's one that's entirely possible with patience, discipline, and the right strategies. Understanding how debt happens and learning from others' experiences can help you avoid common pitfalls and take control of your financial future.

Remember, the journey to debt freedom isn't about perfection. It's about taking consistent steps, making small improvements, and being committed to long-term financial health. Each day you make progress brings you one step closer to a life free of financial worry.

How to Handle Debt Strategically

Debt can be overwhelming, but with a well-thought-out strategy, it's possible to take control and pay it down effectively. The first step is understanding the difference between good debt and bad debt, then choosing a repayment method that works best for your situation.

Understanding Good Debt vs. Bad Debt

The term "debt" often carries a negative connotation, but not all debt is bad. There's a difference between good debt and bad debt, and understanding this distinction can help you manage your finances in a healthier way.

Good Debt: This is debt that helps you build long-term wealth or increase your future earning potential. Examples of good debt include:

- Student loans: Debt taken to invest in your education or skills development.
- Mortgages: Home loans that help you build equity and own a home, an asset that can appreciate over time.
- Business loans: Debt taken to start or grow a business, especially if the business generates more income than the loan payments.

Bad Debt: This is debt that doesn't help you build wealth or increase your earning potential. It often comes with high interest rates and can lead to financial instability. Examples include:

- Credit card debt: Especially when used for non-essential purchases and carried from month to month with high-interest rates.
- Payday loans: Short-term loans with extremely high-interest rates that often trap borrowers in cycles of debt.
- Auto loans for cars that depreciate rapidly: While cars are necessary for many people, taking out loans for vehicles that lose value quickly can be detrimental if the debt isn't managed carefully.

Methods to Pay Off Debt

Once you've identified what kind of debt you're dealing with, it's time to choose a strategy to pay it off. Two of the most widely used strategies are the debt snowball method and the debt avalanche method. Both can be effective, but which one you choose will depend on your personal preferences and financial goals.

1. Debt Snowball Method

The debt snowball method involves paying off your smallest debts first, then using the momentum to tackle larger debts as you go. The idea behind this approach is to build confidence and motivation by quickly eliminating debts.

Here's how it works:

- Make a list of all your debts, ranking them from least to the largest.
- Make minimum payments on the remaining debts while concentrating on paying off the smallest one first.
- Take the money you were paying on the smallest loan and use it to pay off the next smallest debt.
- Continue to do this until you pay off all debts.

Advantages of the Debt Snowball Method:

- Quick wins: Paying off smaller debts first provides immediate progress, which can motivate you to continue.
- Psychological boost: As you eliminate debts, you'll feel more confident and empowered to tackle the next one.

Disadvantages:

- May take longer to save money in the long term, as you might be paying off lower-interest debt before higher-interest debt.

2. Debt Avalanche Method

The debt avalanche method involves focusing on paying off the debt with the highest interest rate first, then moving on to the next highest. This strategy saves you money over time because you're reducing the amount of interest you'll have to pay on your debt.

Here's how it works:

- Make a list of your debts according to interest rate.
- Make the bare minimum payments on the remaining debts and concentrate on paying off the loan with the highest interest rate first.
- Once that debt is paid off, move on to the next highest interest rate debt and repeat the process.

Advantages of the Debt Avalanche Method:

- Saves money on interest: By paying off high-interest debt first, you'll pay less in the long run.
- Efficient: This method tends to be faster in terms of reducing overall debt balances because you're focusing on the most expensive debt first.

Disadvantages:

- No immediate small wins: You may not feel as much progress in the beginning because high-interest debts tend to be larger and take longer to pay off.

Real story

How Julia Paid Off $20,000 in 18 Months

Julia, a single mother and full-time teacher, found herself in a stressful financial situation. She had accumulated $20,000 in credit card debt due to a combination of high medical bills, living expenses, and a few lifestyle splurges. Every month, she struggled to make the minimum payments and watched her balances grow due to high interest rates.

Julia knew she had to take action, but she felt overwhelmed by the sheer size of her debt. She decided to implement the debt avalanche method because she wanted to save as much money on interest as possible. Here's what she did:

List of Debts: Julia took a close look at her debts, which were mainly from two high-interest credit cards, a car loan, and a small personal loan.

- Credit Card 1: $12,000 at 22% interest
- Credit Card 2: $6,000 at 18% interest
- Car Loan: $2,000 at 6% interest
- Personal Loan: $1,000 at 8% interest

Focus on High-Interest Debt: Julia began by directing all of her extra income toward paying off Credit Card 1, while continuing to make the minimum payments on the other debts. Every extra dollar went toward eliminating the high-interest card.

Snowballing Payments: Once Credit Card 1 was paid off in 12 months, Julia used the money she had been paying toward that card to tackle Credit Card 2, then moved on to the next debt on the list.

Cutting Expenses: Julia also made several lifestyle adjustments to free up extra money. She cut out unnecessary subscriptions, cooked more at home, and took on a part-time tutoring job in the evenings. Every dollar she could spare went into paying off her debt.

Achieving Debt Freedom: After 18 months, Julia had completely paid off her $20,000 in debt, with $5,000 in interest savings due to the debt avalanche approach.

Lessons to learn:

- Commitment Is Key: Julia realized that the most important thing was staying committed to her plan. It wasn't easy, but by sticking to her budget and focusing on one debt at a time, she was able to take control of her financial situation.
- Small Adjustments Can Make a Big Difference: Cutting back on little luxuries, like dining out, gave Julia the breathing room she needed to put more money toward her debt.
- The Power of Consistency: By consistently sticking to her debt repayment plan, Julia was able to eliminate her debt faster than she had originally thought possible.

The key to becoming debt-free is adopting a strategy that aligns with your financial goals. Whether you choose the debt snowball or debt avalanche method, consistency is the most important factor. Understand the type of debt you have, choose the right repayment strategy, and make small lifestyle adjustments to free up more money for debt repayment. Like Julia, you can pay off your debt faster than you think and achieve financial freedom.

Staying Debt-Free for the Long Term

Achieving a debt-free life is a monumental step toward financial freedom, but maintaining that freedom requires consistent effort and smart habits.

Building an Emergency Fund

One of the most crucial steps in staying debt-free is building an emergency fund. Life is uncertain, and unforeseen expenses can come up at any time. Without an emergency fund, it's easy to fall back into debt when these situations occur. Whether it's a car repair, a medical bill, or a job loss, having a financial cushion gives you peace of mind and prevents you from relying on credit cards or loans to cover emergencies.

The following is ways to start building your emergency fund:

- Set a Goal: Aim for at least 3 to 6 months' worth of living expenses. This may sound like a lot, but the goal is to ensure that if something unexpected happens, you can cover your basics (housing, food, utilities, etc.) without going into debt.
- Start Small: If the goal seems overwhelming, start with a smaller target. Begin by saving $500 to $1,000. Once that's reached, you can start working toward a more substantial amount.
- Automate Your Savings: Set up automatic transfers from your checking account to a high-interest savings account dedicated to your emergency fund. Even if it's just $50 a month, automating the process makes saving easier and ensures you don't forget.
- Avoid Using It for Non-Emergencies: Your emergency fund is strictly for true emergencies. Resist the temptation to dip into it for non-urgent

expenses, as doing so will only delay your financial security.

Example: Olivia's story is a perfect example of how an emergency fund can save you from going back into debt. A few years ago, Olivia had credit card debt due to unexpected medical bills. She decided to build an emergency fund while paying off her debt. Once she had $1,000 saved up, she felt more secure. When her car broke down unexpectedly, instead of relying on credit cards or loans, she was able to pay for the repair out of pocket, keeping her finances intact.

Avoiding Credit Card Traps

Credit cards are a powerful tool when used responsibly, but they can quickly become a trap if you're not careful. High-interest rates, late fees, and overspending can cause your credit card debt to spiral out of control. To stay debt-free in the long term, it's crucial to manage your credit cards wisely and avoid common traps.

Here are some strategies to avoid falling into the credit card trap:

- Pay Your Balance in Full Each Month: If you can't pay off your balance in full, you're accumulating interest. Try to pay your full balance each month to avoid interest charges. If that's not possible, at least make the minimum payment to avoid penalties.

- Set Spending Limits: Determine how much you can afford to charge to your credit card each month. A good rule of thumb is to spend no more than 30% of your credit limit. If you regularly hit that limit, it's time to reassess your spending habits.

- Avoid Emotional Spending: It's easy to use a credit card as a way to manage stress or emotional discomfort. Emotional spending often leads to buyer's remorse and debt. Before charging something, ask yourself if it's a need or a want, and if you can afford it without relying on credit.

- Track Your Purchases: Regularly track your credit card purchases to ensure you're staying within your budget. Use apps or spreadsheets control your spending. If you notice patterns of overspending in certain areas, take action to adjust your habits.

- Use Credit Cards Wisely: If you can, avoid using credit cards for day-to-day purchases. If you do use them, make sure you have a plan to pay them off quickly. For larger purchases, consider saving up for them instead of using credit.

Example: Take the case of Lisa, who struggled with credit card debt for years due to impulse buying and relying on her credit cards to cover everyday expenses. Once she realized the danger of high-interest credit card debt, she committed to paying off her cards in full each month. She also set a rule for herself: if she couldn't afford something without charging it, she didn't buy it. Lisa now uses her credit cards responsibly, paying off the balance each month, and has stayed debt-free for the past two years.

Building Good Financial Habits

Staying debt-free long-term doesn't just involve managing your credit cards and saving for emergencies—it's about adopting financial habits that keep you on track. Here are some key habits that will help you maintain a healthy financial life:

Track Your Spending: Keeping track of your spending is essential to ensuring you don't overspend and fall into debt. Regularly review your monthly budget and identify areas where you can cut back. If you notice recurring expenses that no longer serve you, eliminate them.

Plan for the Future: Think about your future needs, whether it's retirement, buying a home, or sending your kids to college. Set long-term financial goals and begin saving for them now. The earlier you start, the more prepared you'll be for big life changes and expenses.

Live Below Your Means: One of the most effective ways to avoid falling back into debt is to live below your means. This doesn't mean depriving yourself, but it does mean being mindful about your spending choices. Opt for simple pleasures, make thoughtful purchases, and prioritize your financial goals.

Review and adjust consistently: As life changes, so do your financial priorities. Regularly review your budget, goals, and progress to ensure you're staying on track. Make adjustments when necessary, especially when you experience life changes like a new job, a move, or a change in family circumstances.

Staying debt-free requires a proactive approach. Building an emergency fund, avoiding credit card traps, and developing healthy financial habits are key to maintaining your financial freedom. With dedication, planning, and the right strategies in place, you can safeguard your finances against unexpected setbacks and continue to build wealth for the future. Like Olivia and Lisa, you have the power to stay debt-free and live confidently without the constant stress of financial instability. The key is to remain vigilant, set clear goals, and make choices that align with your long-term financial health.

CHAPTER FIVE

Designing A Life You Love

When it comes to managing your money, it's easy to get caught up in the "must-haves" of life—house payments, bills, and everyday expenses. But designing a life you love involves aligning your money with what truly matters to you. This means identifying your core values and ensuring that your financial choices reflect them.

Here's how to begin:

Determine Your Core Values: Give some thought to what is most important to you. Is it family? Travel? Health? Career growth? Once you identify your values, you can make intentional financial decisions that support them. For example, if health and wellness are important to you, investing in a gym membership or healthy food options might be a top priority.

Create a Spending Plan Based on Your Values: Align your spending with your values by creating a budget that prioritizes what's most important to you. This doesn't mean neglecting your bills or savings; rather, it's about directing your resources toward things that truly enhance your life. If travel is a core value, start setting aside money each month for a vacation fund.

Review Your Financial Habits: Ask yourself whether your current spending habits align with your values. Are you spending money on things that don't truly add value to your life? If so, consider shifting those funds toward more meaningful expenses. For instance, if you spend too much on convenience foods and desire a healthier lifestyle, that's an area where you can reallocate money.

Example: Take Sarah, for example. She was always busy with work and had little time to focus on her health. After recognizing that health was one of her top priorities, she started cutting back on dining out and redirected that money toward a gym membership and healthier food options. The result? Not only did her finances improve, but she felt better both physically and mentally, which boosted her overall happiness.

What a "Dream Life" Looks Like

What does your dream life look like? For some, it's a cozy home with a beautiful garden. For others, it's the freedom to travel the world or have a flexible career that allows for more time with family. The key is defining what your "dream life" truly means. This doesn't have to be a grand, abstract vision; it can be a practical list of goals and desires that bring you joy.

Visualize Your Ideal Life: Spend some time thinking about what would make you happiest. Do you envision yourself debt-free and saving for early retirement? Do you dream of owning a home or launching your own business? Write down these goals and make them tangible. The more specific you are, the easier it will be to work toward them.

Break Down the Big Goals: Once you've defined your dream life, break it down into actionable steps. For instance, if your dream is to travel more, start by researching destinations, setting a travel budget, and planning your time off. For a financial goal, like saving for a down payment on a home, determine how much you need and create a savings plan.

Stay Flexible: Remember, your dream life may evolve over time. As your financial situation changes, your dreams may grow or shift. Stay flexible and adjust your goals as needed while keeping your values front and centre.

Financial Freedom vs. Financial Independence

It's essential to understand the difference between financial freedom and financial independence, as both are significant milestones in designing the life you love. Although the terms are often used interchangeably, they represent distinct concepts.

Financial Freedom: Financial freedom refers to having enough income to cover your living expenses without constantly worrying about money. It means you're in control of your finances, but you might still need to work or actively manage your income streams. It's the ability to live life on your own terms, without the constant pressure of financial insecurity.

Financial Independence: Financial independence takes it a step further. It means you've accumulated enough wealth or income-generating assets that you no longer need to work to support yourself. Your assets (whether it's investments, rental income, or a successful business) cover your living expenses, and you're no longer dependent on an active paycheck.

In short, financial freedom is about having flexibility and peace of mind in your finances, while financial independence is about complete freedom from having to work for money.

Real Story

How Mia Saved for Her Dream Trip While Paying Off Debt

Mia had always dreamed of taking a month-long trip to Europe, but like many, she had student loans, credit card debt, and bills to pay. For years, she thought her dream was out of reach—until she decided to align her finances with her values and take strategic action.

Setting Priorities: Mia started by defining what mattered most to her. She realized that her dream trip was a priority, but so was paying off her debt. She created a plan that balanced both goals. She aimed to pay off her credit card debt within 18 months and set aside money for her trip each month.

Budgeting Smartly: Mia allocated a specific amount toward her debt repayment each month, following the debt snowball method, while simultaneously saving for her trip.

She made small sacrifices, like cooking at home more often and cutting back on unnecessary subscriptions, and used the extra money to fund her savings account.

Finding Extra Income: Mia also leveraged her side hustle, offering freelance graphic design services in her spare time. The extra income from her side business accelerated her ability to pay off debt and save for her trip faster.

After 18 months, Mia had paid off her credit card debt and saved enough money for her dream trip. She spent a month travelling through Europe, enjoying the freedom she had worked so hard to create. She came back with more than just memories—she had the confidence that with the right financial habits, she could continue designing the life she loved.

Designing a life you love requires more than just making money—it's about understanding what's important to you and making sure your money supports those values. Whether it's through creating an emergency fund, prioritizing your dream goals, or distinguishing between financial freedom and independence, aligning your finances with your life's aspirations is the key to long-term happiness. Remember, small steps today can lead to a big, fulfilling future. Like Mia, you have the power to design the life you truly want—one that aligns with your dreams, values, and goals.

Living the Dream Today

Money management isn't just about numbers; it's about creating a life that feels full, balanced, and aligned with your personal values. When you design a budget, it's easy to focus solely on the practical aspects: paying bills, saving for the future, and eliminating debt. But what about joy and fulfilment? Can you include those in your financial planning? The answer is yes.

The Power of Intentional Spending

One of the key aspects of creating a budget that brings you joy is intentional spending. This means making conscious decisions about where your money goes based on what truly brings you happiness and fulfilment. It's not about spending freely on impulse, but about aligning your expenses with your values.

Identify Your Priorities: Take a step back and consider what brings you joy in life. Is it travel, hobbies, or time spent with family and friends? Does investing in personal growth, like education or fitness, make you feel fulfilled? Once you know what truly matters, allocate funds in your budget to reflect these priorities.

Allocate "Joy" Money: Many people focus so much on saving and cutting costs that they forget to plan for joy. Set aside a portion of your budget specifically for things that bring you happiness—whether that's a weekend getaway, a meal at your favourite restaurant, or a class you've been wanting to take. When you know that your budget includes room for joy, you're less likely to feel restricted or deprived.

Small Luxuries Add Up: Joy doesn't always have to come from big-ticket items. In fact, small, intentional luxuries— like a cup of your favourite coffee, a relaxing bath, or a new book—can elevate your everyday experience. These little pleasures, when thoughtfully incorporated into your budget, can make your financial life feel rich and fulfilling.

Reassessing Your Spending: Where Can You Add Value?

Creating space for joy in your budget starts with reassessing where your money is currently going.

Sometimes, we spend on things out of habit or because we think we "should," but these expenses don't always contribute to our happiness. Here's how to make sure you're prioritizing what truly adds value to your life:

Track Your Current Spending: Use an app or simple tracking method to identify where your money is going. Are you spending too much on things that don't bring you happiness—subscriptions, impulse purchases, or eating out frequently? Once you know where the leaks are, you can begin to reallocate funds toward more meaningful expenses.

Cut Back on Non-Essential Spending: Once you've identified areas where you can trim the fat, shift that money into the categories that align with your values. For example, if you're spending too much on subscription services you don't really use, cancel a few and use the savings to fund a course or an activity that brings you joy.

Mindful Consumption: Before purchasing anything, pause and ask yourself if it truly adds value to your life. Will it bring you joy, or is it just a distraction? Mindful spending helps you create a budget that not only covers your needs but also allows for moments of joy and fulfilment.

Reinvesting in Yourself

A big part of creating space for joy is reinvesting in yourself. Whether it's taking time for personal development, pursuing a hobby, or nurturing your health, investing in yourself creates long-term happiness and well-being. Here's how you can incorporate this into your budget:

Invest in Your Health: Health is wealth, and dedicating funds to things like healthy food, fitness classes, or mental health support can increase your overall happiness and productivity. Whether it's a yoga class, meal prep for the week, or a wellness retreat, make sure your budget includes space for health and wellness.

Personal Development: You don't have to spend a fortune to grow. Small investments in books, courses, or learning new skills can be incredibly fulfilling. Whether it's learning how to cook, improve your public speaking, or learn a new language, personal growth pays long-term dividends in both your career and personal life.

Self-Care: Life can be demanding, and self-care is essential for maintaining balance. Include some money for self-care activities that recharge you, whether it's spa treatments, a hobby, or simply time spent alone to reflect and relax.

Stories of Women Who Transformed Their Finances

Creating space for joy within your budget is not just a theoretical exercise—it can make a real difference in your life. Here are the stories of three women who, through intentional budgeting and mindset shifts, transformed their finances while making room for the things that truly mattered to them.

Story 1: Laura's Journey to Financial Freedom and Fulfilment

Laura, a 32-year-old marketing professional, was living paycheck-to-paycheck for years, prioritizing work and neglecting her own happiness. After realizing that her finances were controlling her life rather than the other way around, Laura decided to shift her mindset. She identified what brought her joy: travelling, exploring new cultures, and spending time with loved ones.

With that in mind, she created a new budget that prioritized these passions. She cut back on unnecessary subscriptions, took a more affordable approach to entertainment, and started saving for annual trips. Laura also set aside money for self-care, such as regular spa treatments and fitness classes. In just two years, she paid off debt, saved for her dream vacation, and gained a sense of freedom and fulfilment that she never had before.

Story 2: Emma's Happiness Through Small Sacrifices

Emma's story is a perfect example of how small adjustments can lead to big results. She had always been frugal but found herself feeling deprived, as if her money was being spent only on necessities. Emma decided to make room for joy by focusing on affordable luxuries. She cut down on eating out and shopping for clothes but spent more on cooking classes and weekend getaways with friends. These small changes made a huge difference in her overall happiness. By the end of the year, Emma had not only saved money but had also built stronger relationships and a deeper connection to her passions.

Story 3: Jessica's Balanced Budget and Family Time

Jessica, a single mom, often struggled to balance her finances and the desire to spend quality time with her children. After analyzing her budget, Jessica realized she could save money by reducing her commuting costs and spending more time at home. She reallocated that money to fun family activities like museum trips, board games, and cooking together. These activities brought her family closer, and Jessica felt more fulfilled by the experiences she shared with her children. With a solid budget and a renewed sense of purpose, Jessica found that she could have both financial security and a happy, fulfilling family life.

Designing a budget that includes space for joy and fulfilment is about more than just managing money; it's about living a life that reflects your values and brings you happiness. By focusing on what truly matters, cutting back on non-essential spending, and investing in your personal growth and well-being, you can create financial freedom that serves the life you want to live. Remember, joy doesn't come from just spending money—it comes from using your resources intentionally to build a life that makes you feel alive, balanced, and deeply content.

93 | Catherine Moore

CHAPTER SIX

Avoiding Financial Pitfalls

As women navigate their financial journeys, they often encounter a variety of pitfalls that can derail their progress and create unnecessary stress. Some of these traps are subtle, while others may appear enticing at first. In this chapter, we'll explore three of the most common financial traps that women face: falling for get-rich-quick schemes, overspending on lifestyle inflation, and the temptation to keep up with social media trends. Understanding these traps is crucial for building long-term financial health and avoiding costly mistakes.

Falling for Get-Rich-Quick Schemes

It's easy to dream of sudden wealth—especially when the promise of a quick return is tempting. Whether it's an investment opportunity, a business idea, or a new crypto currency, get-rich-quick schemes are everywhere. They prey on your desire for financial freedom, offering the illusion of an easy way out. But as the saying goes, "If it sounds too good to be true, it probably is."

Why It's Dangerous:

Most get-rich-quick schemes are risky, poorly researched, and often designed to take advantage of those looking for a shortcut to financial security. What seems like a lucrative opportunity often leads to financial loss, emotional stress, and a loss of confidence in your money management abilities.

Signs You Might Be Falling for a Scheme:

- Unclear or overly complicated investment strategies
- Promises of high returns with little to no risk
- Pressure to take immediate action before a chance "disappears"
- A lack of transparency or verifiable track record

Real-Life Example:

Take Sarah's story. Sarah, a 35-year-old teacher, became enamoured with an online investment course promising huge returns on stocks with minimal effort. She invested $10,000, excited by the prospect of early retirement. Unfortunately, the course was poorly designed, and the investment strategy was based on unverified "tips" that led her to lose most of her money. Sarah's desire for fast wealth clouded her judgment, and she learned the hard way that true wealth-building takes time, research, and patience.

How to Avoid It:

- Put your attention on long-term investments with a track record of success
- Be wary of "too good to be true" promises, especially from sources you don't trust
- Always research investment opportunities thoroughly and consult professionals if needed
- Stick to a strategy that aligns with your financial goals, risk tolerance, and values

Overspending on Lifestyle Inflation

The tendency to increase spending as income rises is known as lifestyle inflation. It's easy to fall into the trap of upgrading your lifestyle with each raise or new job, whether it's buying a new car, taking more expensive vacations, or moving into a larger home. While enjoying the fruits of your labour is important, unchecked lifestyle inflation can sabotage your long-term financial goals.

Why It's Dangerous:

When you increase your spending in line with your income, you may find yourself stuck in a cycle of working harder to support a lifestyle that leaves little room for savings or investments. The result? You can end up living paycheck-to-paycheck, even if you're earning more than ever before.

Signs You're Overspending on Lifestyle Inflation:

- Spending more on luxury goods or experiences every time you get a raise
- Feeling pressure to keep up with peers or colleagues who live more lavishly
- Upgrading to bigger or more expensive homes, cars, or other assets without a clear financial plan
- Ignoring savings or investments in favour of immediate gratification

Real-Life Example:

Jessica, a 30-year-old marketing executive, was thrilled when she landed a new job with a higher salary. She immediately upgraded her apartment to a more luxurious place, bought a brand-new car, and started dining out more frequently. Within a year, Jessica's bank account was nearly empty, and her credit card debt had ballooned. She hadn't increased her savings or investments to match her increased income, and her lifestyle was draining her resources faster than she could replenish them. Jessica realized that while she had the means to live well, she hadn't managed her new wealth in a way that would secure her future.

How to Avoid It:

- Pay yourself first by setting aside a portion of your income for savings and investments before spending on non-essential items
- Resist the urge to upgrade your lifestyle every time you get a raise or bonus
- Revisit your financial goals regularly to ensure your spending aligns with your long-term objectives
- Focus on experiences, relationships, and health rather than material possessions

Real Example: How Overspending on "Instagram Lifestyle" Led to Debt

Social media has a powerful influence on how we perceive success and happiness, often equating it with material possessions and experiences. Platforms like Instagram present a curated view of luxury, with influencers showcasing their extravagant lifestyles. For many, this can lead to a desire to "keep up" with the latest trends, whether it's expensive vacations, designer handbags, or dining at trendy spots.

Why It's Dangerous:

Social media often promotes an unrealistic image of what life "should" look like. The pressure to match these ideals can cause you to overspend, especially if you feel like you're falling behind. This can quickly lead to debt and financial strain, as you try to maintain a lifestyle that doesn't align with your actual income or financial goals.

Real-Life Example:

Lisa, a 28-year-old freelance graphic designer, found herself constantly scrolling through Instagram, watching influencers travel to exotic destinations and wear the latest high-end fashion. Influenced by these images, Lisa began spending more on clothing, vacations, and dining out to replicate what she saw online. What started as small splurges turned into larger purchases, and soon Lisa was carrying credit card debt of over $15,000.

She had to confront the reality that keeping up with an Instagram lifestyle was not only draining her finances but also taking a toll on her mental health. Lisa had lost sight of her own financial goals and was caught in a comparison trap.

How to Avoid It:

- Remember that social media shows only a small, organized portion of someone's life, often funded by sponsorships or brand deals
- Focus on creating your own definition of success, based on what truly makes you happy, not what others are posting online
- Practice mindful spending and set boundaries for yourself, especially when it comes to impulse buys or experiences that you can't afford
- Keep your financial goals in mind and align your spending with those goals, not the fleeting desires inspired by social media

Falling into financial traps is common, especially when you're faced with tempting opportunities or pressures to live a certain way. By being aware of the dangers of get-rich-quick schemes, resisting lifestyle inflation, and avoiding the comparison trap of social media, you can make wiser financial decisions that will set you on the path to long-term success. Stay grounded in your financial goals, focus on what truly brings you fulfilment, and remember: it's not about keeping up with others, but about living a life that's financially secure and aligned with your values.

Staying Financially Savvy

Financial scams are on the rise, from phishing emails and investment fraud to identity theft and fake job offers. These schemes often target vulnerabilities, whether it's a lack of financial knowledge or the lure of quick, easy money. Here's how to recognize and protect yourself from scams.

Common Types of Financial Scams:

- Phishing Emails and Texts:
- Fraudsters impersonate legitimate organizations, such as banks or government agencies, to steal your personal information. They often include urgent messages or threatening language to prompt immediate action.

Example: Maria received an email claiming to be from her bank, asking her to update her account details. The email looked authentic, but upon closer inspection, the sender's address was a random sequence of numbers, and the link led to a suspicious website.

Investment Fraud:

These scams promise high returns with little or no risk, preying on those eager to grow their wealth quickly. Fraudsters may create fake companies, use buzzwords like "guaranteed" or "exclusive," and pressure victims into acting immediately.

Online Shopping Scams:

Deals that seem too good to be true—such as luxury items at a fraction of their cost—often result in either counterfeit products or no delivery at all.

Romance Scams:

Scammers form emotional connections with their victims, eventually requesting financial help for fabricated emergencies.

Job or Business Opportunity Scams:

Offers of high-paying remote jobs or franchise opportunities often require upfront payments for "training materials" or "licensing fees."

Red Flags to Watch For:

- Requests for personal information (Social Security numbers, bank details, or passwords)
- Pressure to act quickly or lose an opportunity
- Lack of clear, verifiable information about the organization
- Payment methods like wire transfers, crypto currency, or gift cards

Steps to Protect Yourself:

Verify the Source: Always double-check emails, phone calls, or messages claiming to be from legitimate organizations. Refer to official websites or contact numbers to verify the information.

Educate Yourself: Stay updated on common scam tactics. Organizations like the Federal Trade Commission (FTC) provide resources to help identify fraudulent schemes.

Limit Information Sharing: Be cautious about what you share online, especially on social media, where scammers often mine data.

Use Strong Passwords and Authentication: Protect your accounts with strong passwords and enable two-factor authentication.

Trust Your Instincts: If something feels off, don't proceed until you've done thorough research.

Knowing When to Seek Professional Advice

While financial literacy empowers you to make informed decisions, certain situations call for the expertise of professionals. Whether it's navigating complex tax laws, planning for retirement, or managing significant investments, the right guidance can save you time, stress, and money.

When to Consult a Financial Professional:

Tax Planning and Filing:

Tax laws can be intricate, and mistakes are costly. A tax advisor can help maximize deductions, navigate audits, and create strategies for future savings.

Investment Strategies:

If you're unsure about how to diversify your portfolio, assess risk, or optimize returns, an investment advisor can help.

Retirement Planning:

Setting up retirement accounts, determining how much to save, and understanding withdrawal strategies often require professional insight.

Debt Management:

If you're overwhelmed by debt, credit counsellors can assist with creating repayment plans and negotiating with creditors.

Major Financial Decisions:

Buying a home, starting a business, or preparing an estate plan are scenarios where expertise is invaluable.

How to Choose the Right Professional:

Credentials and Experience:

Look for certifications such as Certified Financial Planner (CFP), Certified Public Accountant (CPA), or Chartered Financial Analyst (CFA).

Fiduciary Duty:

Work with professionals who are legally required to act in your best interest.

Fee Transparency:

Understand how they are compensated—whether through flat fees, commissions, or a percentage of assets managed.

References and Reviews:

Ask for client testimonials or check online reviews.

Long-Term Habits for Financial Safety

Building financial savvy is not a one-time effort—it's a habit. By continuously educating yourself and staying proactive, you can navigate the financial world with confidence.

Ongoing Practices:

- Monitor Your Accounts Regularly: Check your bank and credit card statements for unauthorized transactions.

- Update Your Knowledge: Read financial news, follow trusted experts, and take courses to stay informed.

- Network with Trusted People: Surround yourself with financially responsible individuals who can share insights and advice.

- Create an Emergency Fund: A financial cushion can prevent you from falling into traps during times of stress.

Inspirational Note:

Every dollar you safeguard brings you closer to the life you envision. With vigilance and knowledge, you can confidently sidestep pitfalls and secure your financial future.

By mastering these skills, you'll not only protect your assets but also empower yourself to seize opportunities, build wealth, and live with greater peace of mind.

109 | Catherine Moore

CHAPTER SEVEN

Creating Generational Wealth

Generational wealth refers to financial assets, such as money, property, investments, or businesses, passed down from one generation to the next. It's more than just wealth—it's a means to provide your family with options and opportunities that can break cycles of struggle and build lasting prosperity.

Why It Matters

Breaking the Cycle of Poverty: Generational wealth can give children and grandchildren access to better education, housing, and career opportunities.

Providing Financial Security: A financial safety net can protect your family from unexpected hardships, such as job loss or medical emergencies.

Building a Legacy: It allows you to leave a lasting impact, ensuring your family benefits from your hard work and foresight for years to come.

Steps to Start Building Wealth for the Next Generation

Building generational wealth doesn't require winning the lottery or inheriting riches. With consistent, intentional strategies, you can create a foundation that supports your family's future.

1. Start with Financial Education

Teach yourself and your family about budgeting, saving, investing, and money management. Knowledge is the cornerstone of wealth preservation.

Actionable Tip: Host regular "money talks" with your family to discuss financial goals and strategies.

2. Save and Invest Wisely

While saving is important, investing grows your wealth over time. Use compound interest to your advantage by starting early, even with small amounts.

Actionable Tip: Open investment accounts like 529 plans for college savings or custodial accounts to transfer wealth to minors.

3. Purchase Life Insurance

A life insurance policy ensures your family is taken care of financially in the event of an unexpected loss. It can help pay for education, housing, or other expenses without draining savings.

4. Invest in Real Estate

Real estate is one of the most common ways to pass down generational wealth. Whether it's owning your home or investing in rental properties, real estate often appreciates over time, offering both income and security.

5. Build a Family Business

Starting a family business can create a legacy that continues for generations. Involve your children early to teach them entrepreneurial skills and the value of hard work.

6. Plan Your Estate

Without proper planning, much of your wealth could be lost to taxes or disputes. To guarantee that your assets are dispersed in accordance with your preferences, draft a will and think about establishing a trust.

Actionable Tip: Consult with an estate planner or attorney to create a comprehensive plan.

Real-Life Story

How a Single Mother Built a College Fund for Her Kids

Meet Sarah, a single mother of two. When her youngest child was born, Sarah was working a low-paying job and living paycheck-to-paycheck. The idea of saving for college seemed impossible, but she was determined to give her kids a brighter future.

Step 1: Setting Small, Achievable Goals

Sarah started by opening a 529 college savings plan with just $50 a month. It was a modest beginning, but she knew every little bit counted.

Step 2: Leveraging Side Hustles

To supplement her income, Sarah began freelancing as a writer on weekends. She dedicated half of her earnings from the side hustle to her children's college fund.

Step 3: Teaching Her Kids Financial Responsibility

Sarah involved her kids in the process by teaching them the value of saving. Together, they tracked the college fund's growth, creating a sense of shared commitment.

Step 4: Using Windfalls Wisely

When Sarah received a tax refund, instead of splurging, she deposited a portion into the 529 plan.

The Outcome

By the time her eldest child was ready for college, Sarah had saved $30,000. While it wasn't enough to cover all expenses, it significantly reduced the financial burden on her children and allowed them to graduate with minimal debt.

Sarah's story shows that with determination, small steps, and a clear plan, anyone can build a legacy for the next generation.

Key Takeaways

- Generational wealth is achievable for anyone willing to start, no matter their income level.
- Financial education is the foundation of building and preserving wealth.

- Small, consistent efforts—like saving and investing—can have a significant long-term impact.

Real-life stories like Sarah's demonstrate that starting small can still lead to meaningful results.

By focusing on these principles, you can begin building a brighter, more secure future for your family today.

Estate Planning and Legacy Building

Your financial journey is about ensuring that wealth is preserved and used wisely by the generations that follow. Estate planning and legacy building are crucial steps in creating lasting security and empowering your loved ones to continue building on the foundation you've laid.

Estate planning is often misunderstood as something only the wealthy need, but it's essential for everyone. Whether you have modest savings or significant assets, a well-thought-out plan ensures your wealth is distributed according to your wishes and minimizes disputes or financial hardships for your family.

Why Writing a Will Is Crucial

A will is a legal document that spells out how your assets should be shared after your death. Without a will, the courts will decide on your behalf, which can lead to delays, unnecessary expenses, and family conflicts.

What to Include in a Will:

- Designation of those that will benefit from it (who will receive your assets).
- Guardianship arrangements for minor children.
- Instructions for handling personal possessions and sentimental items.

Common Mistakes to Avoid:

- Not updating your will after major life events like marriage, divorce, or the birth of a child.
- Overlooking digital assets, such as online accounts or crypto-currency.

Actionable Tip: Work with an attorney or use reliable will-writing software to ensure your will is legally valid and comprehensive.

Establishing Trusts for Added Security

A trust is a legal structure in which a trustee is responsible for managing and safeguarding assets for the benefit of designated beneficiaries. Trusts can offer benefits like reducing estate taxes, avoiding probate, and providing financial oversight for heirs who may lack money management skills.

Types of Trusts:

Revocable Living Trust: Allows you to retain control of your assets during your lifetime and specify how they're distributed after your death.

Irrevocable Trust: Offers more tax benefits but requires relinquishing control over the assets placed in the trust.

Real-Life Example: A grandmother creates a trust to ensure her grandchildren's education is funded without giving them unrestricted access to large sums of money.

Educating the Next Generation on Financial Literacy

Leaving wealth without financial education can lead to its rapid depletion. Educating your heirs ensures they understand how to manage and grow the resources you've worked so hard to build.

Why Financial Literacy Matters

Studies show that individuals who receive financial education are more likely to make sound decisions about saving, investing, and debt management. This knowledge empowers them to maintain and expand generational wealth.

Start Early: Introduce financial concepts to children through age-appropriate lessons, such as budgeting with allowance money or saving for a toy.

Be Transparent: Share insights into your financial planning to normalize discussions about money.

Ways to Teach Financial Literacy

Set Up Savings Challenges: Encourage children or grandchildren to save for a goal, matching their contributions to show the value of disciplined saving.

Explain Investment Basics: Use simple examples like growing a garden to illustrate how investments can grow over time.

Provide Access to Resources: Share books, podcasts, or workshops on personal finance.

Creating a Legacy of Responsibility

Beyond teaching financial skills, instil values like generosity and responsibility. Encourage heirs to think about how they can use wealth to make a positive impact, whether through charitable giving, community projects, or supporting family members in need.

Key Takeaways

- Estate planning allows you to dictate how your assets are distributed while reducing stress and uncertainty for your loved ones.
- Writing a will and establishing trusts are essential components of a solid estate plan.
- Financial literacy equips the next generation with the tools to manage and grow wealth, preserving your legacy.

By combining thoughtful planning with education, you can create a foundation that benefits your family for years to come.

Take action today to secure your legacy and empower your loved ones with the knowledge and resources they need to thrive.

CHAPTER EIGHT

Your Financial Wellness Journey

Your journey toward financial wellness requires not only knowledge but also action.

Before diving into numbers and strategies, take a moment to dream. How do you see financial freedom in your life? Whether it is owning your dream home, travelling the world, or simply feeling secure, it's essential to connect your goals with your values.

Guided Exercise:

Imagine Your Ideal Life: Write down five key things you'd want to achieve if money were no obstacle.

S/NO	THINGS TO ACHIEVE
1.	
2.	
3.	
4.	
5.	

Prioritize Your Goals: Rank them by importance and feasibility.

RANK	IMPORTANT AND FEASIBLE GOALS
1.	
2.	
3.	
4.	
5.	

Break It Down: For each goal, identify smaller steps you can start taking today.

RANK	IMPORTANT AND FEASIBLE GOALS	SMALLER STEPS TO TAKE
1.		
2.		
3.		
4.		
5.		

Goal-Setting Templates

Goals give you direction. Use these templates to create meaningful and actionable financial goals:

SMART Goal Framework

Specific: State exactly what you want to accomplish (e.g., save $10,000 for a down payment).

Measurable: Attach numbers to your goals so you can track progress.

Achievable: Be realistic about what you can accomplish within your timeline.

Make sure your goals reflect your core values and support your long-term aspirations.

Time-Bound: Set a deadline to create urgency.

Template Example:

S/N	GOAL	TIMELINE	MONTHLY TARGET
1.	Build a $5,000 emergency fund	12 months	Save $417 per month
2.			
3.			
4.			
5.			

Action Plan:

- Arrange automatic transfers to a high-yield savings account to grow your savings effortlessly.
- Reduce dining out expenses by $100 monthly.
- Take on freelance work to earn an extra $300 a month.

Budget Planning Worksheets

Budgeting is the cornerstone of financial wellness. Use these worksheets to create a budget that works for you.

Basic Budget Template

Category	Planned Amount	Actual Amount	Difference
Income			
Fixed Expenses			
Savings/Investments			
Variable Expenses			
Total			

Categories to Consider:

- Fixed Expenses: Rent, utilities, insurance, loan payments.
- Savings: Emergency fund, retirement, vacation fund.
- Variable Expenses: Groceries, transportation, entertainment.

Debt-Tracking Charts

Eliminating debt is a major milestone on your journey to financial wellness. Use these charts to track your progress and stay motivated.

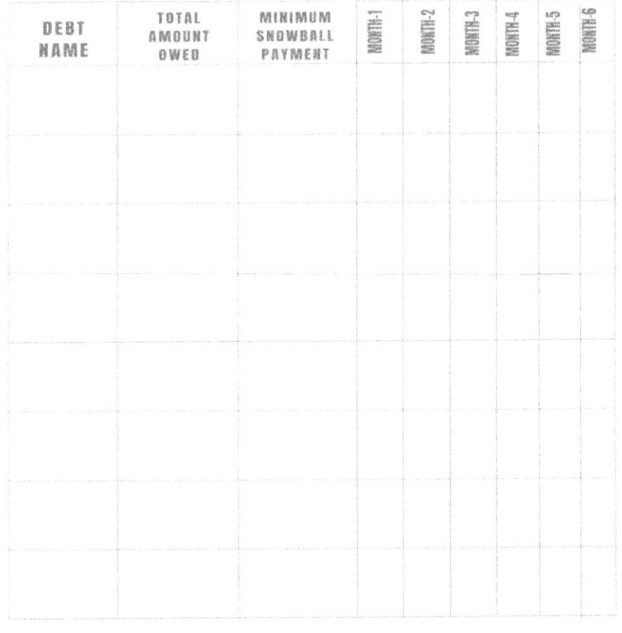

DEBT SNOWBALL WORKSHEET

DEBT NAME	TOTAL AMOUNT OWED	MINIMUM SNOWBALL PAYMENT	MONTH-1	MONTH-2	MONTH-3	MONTH-4	MONTH-5	MONTH-6

DEBT AVALANCHE METHOD CHART

DEBT NAME	TOTAL BALANCE	INTEREST RATE	MONTHLY PAYMENT	REMAINING BALANCE

Key Takeaways

- Dream Big: Allow yourself to envision a life of financial freedom and use that vision to fuel your motivation.

- Stay Organized: Goal-setting templates and tracking tools keep your progress visible and manageable.
- Adapt As Needed: Your financial situation may change, but these tools can grow with you.

This workbook is designed to be your companion, guiding you from where you are now to where you want to be. Start filling it in today—the first step is always the most empowering.

Reflect and Celebrate Progress

Achieving financial wellness is as much about the journey as the destination. Along the way, it's essential to pause, reflect on your progress, and celebrate your victories, no matter how small. This practice not only keeps you motivated but also helps build a positive relationship with money. Let's explore how to reflect meaningfully and celebrate your financial achievements.

Writing Your Financial Affirmations

The way you think about money can significantly influence your financial success. Affirmations—positive, focused statements—can help you shift limiting beliefs and stay aligned with your goals.

What Are Financial Affirmations?

Financial affirmations are empowering phrases that reinforce your confidence and keep your financial goals in focus. They are a way to remind yourself of your potential and progress.

Examples of Financial Affirmations:

- "I am capable of managing my finances effectively."
- "Every little step I take brings me very close to financial freedom."
- "I spend my money on things that align with my values."
- "I am building a protective future for myself and my family."

Tips for Writing Effective Affirmations:

- Make Them Personal: Use language that feels natural and relevant to your life.

- Example: "I'm building my emergency fund one step at a time."
- Focus on the Positive: Frame affirmations in terms of what you want to achieve, not what you're avoiding.
- Instead of: "I won't spend recklessly," say, "I make mindful spending decisions."
- Be Specific: Tie your affirmations to tangible goals. Example: "I save $200 each month to grow my vacation fund."

How to Incorporate Affirmations:

- Write your affirmations in a dedicated journal.
- Post them where you'll see them daily, like on your mirror or desk.
- Repeat them to yourself each morning or evening to reinforce your mindset.

Celebrating Small Wins on Your Journey

Financial success doesn't happen overnight—it's a series of small, consistent steps. Celebrating these milestones is an essential part of maintaining motivation and building confidence.

The Power of Celebration:

Reinforces Progress: Acknowledging even minor achievements reminds you of your capabilities.

Keeps You Motivated: Celebrations act as a reward for your hard work.

Builds Positive Momentum: Recognizing success helps sustain good financial habits.

Ideas for Celebrating Small Wins:

For Paying Off Debt: Treat yourself to a favourite meal or a day out.

For Reaching a Savings Milestone: Allow yourself a small splurge on something meaningful.

For Sticking to Your Budget: Enjoy a relaxing activity, like a movie night at home.

Example:

When Rachel hit her goal of saving $500 for emergencies, she celebrated by buying a book she'd been eyeing. This small reward kept her excited to save for her next milestone.

Reflection Questions:

- What progress am I sure I've made toward my goals this month?
- How can I celebrate without derailing my financial plans?
- What did I learn from this achievement that can help with future goals?

Key Takeaways

- Affirmations are a powerful tool for maintaining a positive money mindset.
- Acknowledging small successes helps maintain motivation and strengthens positive habits.
- Reflecting on your progress helps you stay connected to your financial goals.
- Take time to recognize how far you've come, celebrate your successes, and continue building a financial future that you're proud of.

133 | Catherine Moore

CONCLUSION

Congratulations on taking this journey toward financial wellness! By reaching this point in the book, you've proven one vital truth: you are committed to creating a brighter financial future.

This journey hasn't been about flawlessness—it's been about making progress. From understanding your relationship with money to learning how to build wealth, avoid debt traps, and align your finances with your dreams, every step you've taken has brought you closer to your goals.

Your Path to Financial Wellness

Financial wellness isn't a one-time achievement; it's a continuous process of learning, adapting, and growing. It's about making choices that align with your values, prioritizing your goals, and taking control of your financial future.

Remember:

- It's Never Too Late to Start: Whether you're starting fresh or refining your strategies, every positive action counts.

- Small Steps Matter: Big changes often begin with small, consistent efforts.

- Your Money, Your Rules: Designing a life you love starts with understanding what truly matters to you.

The tools, strategies, and stories in this book are to empower you to take control of your finances with confidence. Use what you've learned to create a plan that works for your unique life and aspirations.

You have everything it takes to succeed. Financial independence and security aren't reserved for a select few—they are achievable for anyone willing to learn, plan, and take action.

Mistakes will happen, and challenges may arise, but every setback is an opportunity to learn and grow stronger. Celebrate every win, no matter how small, and remind yourself how far you've come.

As you continue on this journey, keep these words in mind:

- You are capable.

- You are worthy of abundance.
- Your financial wellness is within your reach.

This is your story, your journey, and your opportunity to create a life of freedom, security, and joy. Go forward with confidence—because you've got this.

www.ingramcontent.com/pod-product-compliance
Lightning Source LLC
Chambersburg PA
CBHW071031240526
45469CB00006BD/2172